LOVE

AROUND

THE

WORLD

FLEUR PIERETS

Illustrated by

FATINHA RAMOS

SIXFOOTPRESS

HOUSTON

My name is Fleur. I know, it's a bit of a weird name.

It means "flower" in French, because my mother wanted me to blossom.

Julian is the name of my love.

We live together, eat together, sleep together, and work together.

Julian is a woman. Just like me.

One day I went down on one knee
and asked Julian to marry me.

Getting married is a big step in life.

"Yes!" she said. "I want to spend the
rest of my life with you. And you're going
to look amazing in a wedding dress!"

Julian and I found out that getting married was not going to be easy.

In most countries, a man cannot marry a man and a woman cannot marry a woman.

There are 195 countries in the world, but we could only get married in 28 of them. We thought this was unfair.

"Would you like to marry me in all 28 countries?" asked Julian. I said, "Yes!"

And so our adventure began.

We packed one suitcase each. Some books, some clothes, and our favorite bunny.

And we started to fight for a better future.
For equal rights for all people.

And for love. Lots of love.

Julian was born in the Netherlands.

Same-sex marriage was not allowed when she was a little girl.

In 2011, the first official gay wedding in the world took place in Amsterdam.

For Julian, it was a childhood dream come true.

In New York City, in the **United States**, people were proud to allow same-sex marriage.

We gave almost a hundred interviews, but we never got tired of telling our story. Two women traveling the world to get married was big news.

Every summer, Brazil's gay community and all of their friends come to the streets to celebrate equal rights. They speak out for all people to feel safe, because feeling safe is important.

The celebrations are called Pride. After our wedding ceremony in São Paulo, we celebrated Pride with more than 3 million people.

Julian and I always hold hands, day and night.

In **Australia**, we held hands during the smoking ceremony, an ancient custom among the Aborigines, the first people to live in the country.

The smoke is believed to have healing powers and to bring good luck.

As we traveled from one country to the next, we passed many countries where it was forbidden for us to get married. But not France, where we married in Paris, the most romantic city in the world.

When I met Julian, I told my mother I fell in love with a girl.

"As long as you are happy," she said.

At the wedding in Belgium, where I grew up, my mother clapped the loudest.

I am very proud to have a mom who loves and cares for me.

Not every family is the same. Some families have a mommy and a daddy. Others have two mommies or two daddies. Some have just one mom or dad. In **Ireland**, they understood that the most important thing was to make sure Irish children are loved and cared for, regardless of how many mommies and daddies they have.

"Do you know how much I love you?"

Julian often asked me.

"How much?"

"If you go from here to the nearest star, and then you hop to all the other stars, and before you come back to Portugal, you spin several times around the planet Earth. That's how much I love you!" she said.

In every country we visited, people welcomed us with open arms.

In **Canada**, they are proud of their country, where they can be themselves and feel safe.

In a world where it's not always easy to express yourself, it's important to find who you truly are.

In Spain, we met Dolores, an elderly woman dressed in black. Her back was so stooped, it looked like she could tip over any minute.

We asked Dolores if we could get married in Spain, which is a very religious country.

"Of course you can," Dolores said.
"God doesn't make mistakes."

In Iceland, the sun shines day and night during the summer.
After our wedding in Reykjavík we danced all night in the midnight sun.

In **Finland**, we became friends with a designer named Touko and his husband, Veli.

They told us that in their country, the custom is for the bride to wear white.

Julian chose to wear white pants and I wore a beautiful white wedding dress.

In Mexico, we were entwined in beautiful orange blossoms. This symbolizes unity according to Mexican tradition.

Julian and I were in the middle of our adventure, and she asked me if I wanted to marry her in the next 15 countries.

Every day I love her more, so what do you think I said?

Fleur Pierets is an artist, writer, and speaker who focuses on gay identity and positive activism.

Together with her late wife, Julian P. Boom, she founded *Et Alors?* magazine. It features conversations with queer musicians, visual artists, writers, and performers by whom they are inspired, capturing a world striving for change and awareness of gay imagery and female representation in art history.

In 2017, Fleur and Julian started 22–The Project, a performance-art piece in which the couple would marry in every country that legalized same-sex marriage. There were 22 countries when they launched the project in 2017; since then, the number of countries has grown to 28.

After wedding #4, in France, Julian was diagnosed with brain cancer. She died shortly thereafter. With this book series, Fleur is seeing their project through to the end.

www.etalorsmagazine.com
www.jfpierets.com
www.22theproject.com

PHOTO: DUNCAN DE FEY